WHO THE HELL DO *I* THINK *I* AM?

A
B R I E F
A N D
C A N D I D
A S S E S S M E N T
O F
O N E S E L F

TIMON KYLE DURRETT

TIMON KYLE DURRETT

ISBN:1505460212

PHOTO: TARJI MICHELLE SMEDLEY

DEDICATION

To my wonderful sons, my family and friends, The Bruhs,
and everyone who has offered love and light;
and
In Loving Memory of my mother Katherine Durrett and
my brother Bryant Leshea Pretlow, who both taught me
many invaluable lessons.

CONTENTS

CONTENTS

HOŌ Đə
HEL DOŌ
AHY
ƟI NG K
AHY AM?

FROM THE AUTHOR

The desk clock read 7:48 when I woke up that Sunday morning. After a light breakfast and a brisk workout, I decided to relax a bit. So, I turned on the television and thumbed through a couple of my favorite magazines during commercial breaks.

Then something hit me.

I looked at the people on the screen and on the pages: actors, directors, writers, architects, composers, recording artists, scientists, illustrators, computer programmers, inventors, speakers, clothing designers, athletes, etc., all whom I considered great.

I thought, Wow, they're really doing big things.

As I sat there staring at the television and holding the magazine, a solemn feeling came over me. Not because I did not have the things those great people had or because I was not where they were in life. It was because I realized where I could and should be in my life, where I would be had I applied myself and focused more.

I thought of all the time I had squandered, that I did not invest into my ideas, my dreams, and my future.

I wished that I could go back in time and fashion my life after those people I so admired.

Instead of wishing and hoping my life would turn around, I should be doing. Right now, I should be actively fashioning my life, not after theirs, but after all the thoughts and dreams I had about how I want it to be.

At that moment, I realized that I could do more.

So, I decided to make a difference in my life.

My thoughts went from solemn to inspired, desirous and impassioned ideas for significant change. I put down the magazines, turned off the television, stood in front of my bathroom mirror, and asked:

"What are you doing with your life, Timon?"
"Are you satisfied with it?"
"What are your biggest dreams?"
"Have you reached them?"

"What can you do RIGHT NOW to get closer to them?"

I had answers for these questions and many others. Then one question struck a major chord:

"Who The Hell Do I Think I Am?"

I did not have an answer.

I knew what I wanted, what I hoped, wished and dreamed for, but I did not know Who The Hell I Was. I looked at my reflection for what seemed like hours. Then, I took a personal inventory. I actually wrote it down. I analyzed who I had become up to that point. What I thought about the most. What I was doing to myself.

What I wasn't doing for myself.

Why I was or wasn't doing it.

At first, I shunned anything negative that came to mind. Then I asked myself another question: "Why are you doing that?"

For far too long, I was trying to convince myself of things about me that were not true.

I came up with reasons, justifications, substantiations, etc., all to make me comfortable. I told myself that I was happy, that I was strong, and that I was being honest with myself. These were all untruths. Cushions I created as protection from any adverse feelings about the consequences of my actions, for which I would blame outward stimuli.

Of course, my exterior environment, atmosphere, surroundings, etc., played some part. But how could I place outright and total blame on any outward stimuli for something that I chose to do?

I had made a bed of untruths and I was comfortable lying in it. I did not want to face my actuality because it did not make me feel good. Moreover, I did not want people to see me as I truly saw myself. I used whatever social acceptance I had gained as a way to create a false sense of self-worth. Through the opinions of others - whether they were of praise or ridicule - I had fabricated validations for qualities I did not yet possess.

I tried to bury all the unfavorable things I had known about myself, but never wanted to face because facing the truth took a certain level of responsibility that I did not want. It took an amount of courage that I did not have.

But that Sunday I dug deep, embraced the responsibility, found the courage, and faced myself with brutal honesty.

TIMON KYLE DURRETT

Right then, I realized that I was the product of my mental environment. What I thought was what I lived. Whether I wanted to admit it or not, that was my truth. I was responsible for my every circumstance.

Things did not happen to me; I made things happen by way of my choices, which, of course, were brought about by my thoughts; the very thoughts that led to the outcome of my life leading right up to that Sunday morning.

And for that reason, I had to hold myself accountable for the path my life had taken. It was a pivotal moment, one that changed everything.

When I came to that moment of realization and began to tell myself the truth, I felt like a new person. My thoughts instantly transformed into passionate desires. My perspective was changed instantly and I liked what I saw. People, events, conditions in my life, they all started to look different. Things I once considered burdens were really blessings.

Incidents I thought to be stumbling blocks were actually stepping-stones. Matters I viewed as setbacks were, in fact, set ups for success.

I was exhilarated because I had finally accepted a truth that, for so long, was locked away inside me. A truth that had grown so tired of being suffocated, it broke free and made itself known to me. I decided to regain control of my life, to take charge of it, and make it a worthwhile existence that I could be proud of. I desired a change for the better and there was nothing that was going to stop me from making that change.

I recalled the people on the television and in those

those who DO NOT. And those who DO also THINK, PLAN and ACT.

With that conclusion, I grabbed my laptop, locked myself in my office, and began writing the very words that you now read.

As I wrote, I referred to my personal inventory. One factor to which I paid closest attention was that with certain plans of action – some of which were of greater importance than I may have admitted.

I would start out strong, continue in a weak manner, and then never finish. That was because I would spend more time guessing, hoping, wishing, and questioning than I would spend desiring, thinking, planning and doing. So, to transmute my newfound mindset into tangible results, I not only thought about the life I desired, I acted upon those thoughts as soon as I conceived them.

And whether the task at hand was large or small, I kept acting on it until I reached a definitive goal. By continually assigning goal-oriented actions to my conscious thought and planning, I have ultimately adopted the overall philosophy expressed in this work.

And it has, without a doubt, proven life changing.

So, do your life a favor. Go stand in front of a mirror, take a long, hard look at whom you see, and ask the question on the cover of this book.

Now ask again. This time, make certain that you are completely honest when you answer. Not that you have a choice, of course. Of all the people you know, there is one to whom you cannot lie: YOURSELF. And even if you could, why would you want to? There are plenty of people mind, heart and soul with all sorts of lies.

They would do their best to make you believe gazillions of life-stifling untruths about yourself. So, why do to yourself what others are more than willing to do to you? Think about that one for a minute.

So, got an answer that truthfully and accurately DEFINES you, yet? If not, keep asking. It will come to you. But if you do have an answer, are you satisfied with it? Does it make you happy? Does it make you proud? Does it make you want to hold your head high, walk with confidence, unashamed to proclaim to the world who and how you are right now? If so, then maybe you should put down this book, never pick it up again, and go on with your life.

Or does your answer make you want to conceal yourself, or urge you to hang your head in humility and continue on that long, congested road of self-loathing? If it does, what is your plan? How impassioned are you about profoundly enhancing and advancing your life?

WHAT AM I WILLING TO DO TO CHANGE MY ANSWER?

Think about that one for a minute, too.

Of course, if you are not satisfied with your answer and you still do not care to make any changes, you can just sit right where you are and continue to do what millions have grown accustomed to doing: NOTHING.

That would be easiest, would it not, to do absolutely NOTHING? I mean, come on. Seriously. Who wants to put forth any effort to be better, happier, stronger, faster,

W T H D I T I A

Not you, right? Or *do* you?

If you do, good.

Keep reading.

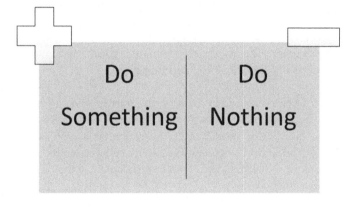

INTRODUCTION

Often times, the truth can be very ugly. So ugly, in fact, that most people cannot bear the thought of facing it. Instead, we turn away from it and fabricate a facsimile of ourselves. We highly idealize our looks, weight, health, productivity, finances, achievements, social acceptance, relationships, personalities, and our lives.

When you stood in front of that mirror - which I hope you did - and asked the reflection "WHO THE HELL DO I THINK I AM?" and answered it as frankly as you asked, you began a journey to self-discovery, self-awareness, self-discipline, self-reliance, self-confidence, and self-improvement.

And from where does all this "self" stuff originate? The Mind. Our thoughts influence our words, our words influence our actions, our actions our habits, our habits our character, and our character our destinies. The mind is where thoughts are born.

Thereafter, we either nurture or neglect them. And depending on the thought, both the neglect and nurturing can either be helpful or harmful. So, why not conceive positive thoughts that generate affirmative words, which prompt resolute action, leading to fruitful habits, fashioning a first-rate character that forges an extraordinary destiny?

As you read on, if something happens to push a

attention. This book is not some promise to give your life a total makeover. It is simply a concise, plainspoken, straightforward, matter-of-fact, right-in-my-face, first-person evaluation, critique, and fortifier of its reader.

So, if it is somewhere in you - whether just below the surface or deep down to the marrow - to be unreservedly honest with yourself, then after reading this you just may see the need for that makeover.

So, let me ask myself...

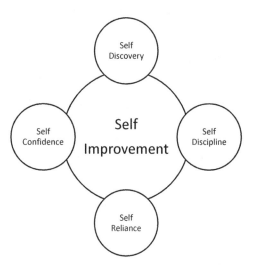

TIMON KYLE DURRETT

1
HOW DO I START MY DAY?

What is my daily foundation?

What is the underlying basis or principle that, once acted upon, will make today gainful and effective? DESIRE.

It is my life-long, undying desire that, in some way, drives me every moment of every day. My desire is the passion of my spirit connecting with my physical reality. It is the fusion of that for which I thirst and the action it takes to attain it.

So, today I move away from my comfort zone and closer to my dreams. Today, I let go of any small thinking, focus on that desire, and allow it to usher me to unbelievable heights.

I start everyday with my DESIRE.
It drives me.

However...

DE·SIRE· | Dəˈzī(ə)R |
VERB

NOUN
A STRONG FEELING OF WANTING
TO HAVE SOMETHING OR WISHING
FOR SOMETHING TO HAPPEN.

VERB
STRONGLY WISH FOR OR WANT
(SOMETHING).

2
"DO I EXERCISE DAILY?"

Jogging on a treadmill for 45 minutes or attending an aerobics class after work three days a week is great. Yet, physical exercise alone is not enough. I must exercise MY MIND as well.

I WILL EXERCISE MY MENTAL POWER to summon innovative, strategic, and penetrating concepts. I WILL EXERCISE MY MENTAL POWER to select assuring thoughts and envision magnificent dreams.

I will do this each and every day. How?

By meditating on my most engrossing desires, goals, and ideas for at least 30 minutes a day; by writing those desires down and putting them in places where I'm sure to see them throughout my day; and by committing my writings to memory and formulating a daily mantra that I repeat as often as I can remember.

W T H D I T I A

EX·ER·CISE |ˈEKSəRˌSĪZ|
VERB

- USE OR APPLY (A FACULTY, RIGHT,
OR PROCESS).

POW·ER |ˈPOU(-ə)R|
NOUN

- THE ABILITY TO DO SOMETHING
OR ACT IN A PARTICULAR WAY, ESP.
AS A FACULTY OR QUALITY.

TIMON KYLE DURRETT

My mind is like a muscle.

It appreciates the rigors I put it through. It welcomes the discipline. The more I use, exercise, and challenge it, the keener, sharper, stronger, and more useful it becomes, allowing me the capacity to zero in on my DESIRE.

So, I will train my mind everyday to do more for me than it did the day before. And to show its gratitude, it will work in ways I never imagined possible.

I exercise my mind on a daily basis. Now...

W T H D I T I A

KEEN |KĒN|
ADJECTIVE

- HAVING OR SHOWING
EAGERNESS OR ENTHUSIASM.

- SHARP OR PENETRATING, IN
PARTICULAR (OF MENTAL FACULTIES)
QUICK TO UNDERSTAND OR
FUNCTION.

3
"WHO AM I TO ME?"

What am I saying to me about me? I have to be totally forthright with myself on this one because what I say to myself about myself when I am by myself determines MY SELF-ESTEEM.

What I plant in my mind is what will grow and flourish. So, I must be sure to cultivate the right mental crops. If I plant an apple seed in the soil, I cannot expect a grapevine to grow, can I?

If I do not feed my mind affirmative thoughts, it will gorge upon any useless garbage that finds its way in. Therefore, I cannot expect to be positive and productive if I continually allow adverse and unfavorable thoughts to filter into, and remain in, my head. With all things in life, what I put into it is precisely what I will get out of it.

If I dip a sponge into a bucket of water, I would be a fool to imagine that when I take it out and squeeze it I will get wine. MY internal conversation becomes MY external manifestation.

W T H D I T I A

SELF-ES·TEEM |SELF I'STĒM|
NOUN

- CONFIDENCE IN ONE'S OWN
WORTH OR ABILITIES; SELF-RESPECT.

AF·FIRM·ATIVE
|əˈFəRMəTIV|
ADJECTIVE

- SUPPORTIVE, HOPEFUL, OR
ENCOURAGING.

TIMON KYLE DURRETT

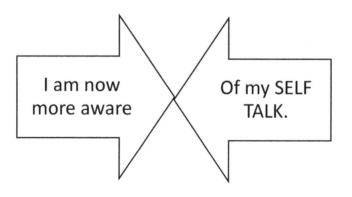

I am now more aware

Of my SELF TALK.

W T H D I T I A

CUL·TI·VATE |ˈKəLTəˌVĀT|
VERB

- TRY TO ACQUIRE OR DEVELOP (A
QUALITY, SENTIMENT, OR SKILL).
- APPLY ONESELF TO IMPROVING
OR DEVELOPING (ONE'S MIND OR
MANNERS).

PRO·DUC·TIVE |PRəˈDəKTIV; PRŌ-|
ADJECTIVE

- ACHIEVING OR PRODUCING A
SIGNIFICANT AMOUNT OR RESULT.
- PRODUCING OR GIVING RISE TO.

4
"WOULD I SPEND TIME WITH ME IF I WEREN'T ME, AND DO I TAKE OWNERSHIP OF MY LIFE?"

Am I a source of enjoyment, or am I a source of displeasure, causing ill feelings and angst? Do I reflect the remarkable, life-changing qualities I see in those I admire, or am I a habitual, day-to-day complainer who is among the exponentially growing number of people who cry out, "WOE IS ME?"

If I am the type described in the latter portion of these two questions, then I may be considered an IRRITANT and a VICTIM. It has been said that irritants have one principal distinction: NOBODY WANTS THEM AROUND.

So, what good is it to be in the presence of individuals who offer nothing more than annoyances?

WTHDITIA

MIS·ERY |ˈMIZ(ə)RĒ|
NOUN
- A STATE OR FEELING OF GREAT
DISTRESS OR DISCOMFORT OF MIND
OR BODY.

LA·ZY |ˈLĀZĒ|
ADJECTIVE
- UNWILLING TO WORK OR USE
ENERGY, CHARACTERIZED BY LACK
OF EFFORT OR ACTIVITY, SHOWING A
LACK OF EFFORT OR CARE,
SLOW-MOVING.

It has also been said that victims possess a key characteristic: THEY DO NOT TAKE OWNERSHIP OF THEIR LIVES.

They are known for blaming everyone and everything else for their circumstances, routinely making a fuss about matters over which they usually have total control. Powerful, self-assured people loathe the victim mentality.

But there is a support group that will unfailingly pacify and sympathize with the notorious grousing victim. That group: OTHER VICTIMS.

They have been known to take delight in complaining to, with, and about one another. Two things about complaining: IT DOES NOT HELP ANYTHING and NOBODY WANTS TO HEAR IT; at least not the strong-minded and influential.

Complaining has been likened to misery, and MISERY IS LAZY AND CONTAGIOUS!

It loves to wallow in unhappiness and feel sorry for itself. It prefers to moan and groan about its undesirable situations instead of changing them.

WTHDITIA

IR·RI·TANT |ˈIRITəNT|
NOUN

- THING THAT IS CONTINUALLY
ANNOYING OR DISTRACTING.

VIC·TIM |ˈVIKTəM|
NOUN

- A PERSON WHO IS TRICKED OR
DUPED INTO BELIEVING OR
ACCEPTING SOMETHING
UNDESIRABLE.

TIMON KYLE DURRETT

Misery would rather bask in the pity showered upon it than eliminate the very thing that presumably makes it pitiful. Misery not only loves company, it loves company more miserable than itself. And if it is not in that company, it will latch on to anyone it can and try to make him or her exactly like itself.

I AM NEITHER MISERABLE, NOR AM I LAZY! I TAKE FULL RESPONSIBILITY FOR MY LIFE. That being so, I DO NOT COMPLAIN because I AM NOT A VICTIM and, therefore, AM NOT AN IRRITANT.

I conduct myself with a shining attitude, pleasant behavior, and an admirable posture. I show others how to regard me, and thusly how to conduct themselves around me.

This leads to my continually being surrounded only by radiant people who enjoy my presence, who will encourage me to shine brighter, and who motivate me to live a life of which I happily take ownership.

Hmmm. Ok. I am pretty sure I would spend time with me, but there is always room for growth. So…

W T H D I T I A

PLEAS·ANT |ˈPLEZəNT|
ADJECTIVE

- GIVING A SENSE OF HAPPY
SATISFACTION OR ENJOYMENT.
- (OF A PERSON OR THEIR
MANNER) FRIENDLY AND
CONSIDERATE.

AD·MI·RA·BLE |ˈADMəRəBəL|
ADJECTIVE

- AROUSING OR DESERVING
RESPECT AND APPROVAL.

RA·DI·ANT |ˈRĀDĒəNT|
ADJECTIVE

- (OF A PERSON OR THEIR
EXPRESSION) CLEARLY EMANATING
GREAT JOY, LOVE, OR HEALTH.

- (OF AN EMOTION OR QUALITY)
EMANATING POWERFULLY FROM
SOMEONE OR SOMETHING; VERY
INTENSE OR CONSPICUOUS.

5
"WHERE IS THE FIRST PLACE I LOOK FOR CHANGE?"

As often as I like, I can change my clothes, shoes, hairstyle, and even my mind. But it is a phenomenal thing to realize that I can change my life by changing my mindset.

Mindset changes that are of greatest consequence are those made of four chief facets of my life: my MORALS, that which I believe to be right or wrong; my STANDARDS, that which I demand of myself; my VALUES, that which I cherish; and my DESIRES, that which I want more than anything.

If I truly desire to change these aspects of my life – whether one or all four – there is only one place for me to look first: inside ME. I am not my circumstances; I am the maker and changer of them.

TIMON KYLE DURRETT

RE·AL·IZE |ˈRĒ(ə)ˌLĪZ|
VERB

- BECOME FULLY AWARE OF
(SOMETHING) AS A FACT;
UNDERSTAND CLEARLY.

- CAUSE (SOMETHING DESIRED OR
ANTICIPATED) TO HAPPEN.

CHANGE | CH ĀNJ|
VERB

- MAKE OR BECOME DIFFERENT.

- MAKE OR BECOME A DIFFERENT
SUBSTANCE ENTIRELY; TRANSFORM.

- GIVE UP (SOMETHING) IN
EXCHANGE FOR SOMETHING ELSE.

WTHDITIA

Therefore, my circumstances do not make ME. They reflect ME. Simply put, change starts WITHIN, not WITHOUT.

So, I will dig deep within myself and seek out that which I desire to change. Day and night, I will focus so intensely on these changes until they become habits.

I see the change(s) that need(s) to be made and I am acting accordingly!

Now...

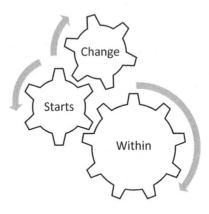

TIMON KYLE DURRETT

MIND-SET
NOUN

- THE ESTABLISHED SET OF
ATTITUDES HELD BY SOMEONE.

WITH·IN |WIÐˈIN; WIˈƟ-|
PREPOSITION

INSIDE (SOMETHING).
- INSIDE THE RANGE OF (AN AREA
OR BOUNDARY).

- INSIDE THE RANGE OF (A
SPECIFIED ACTION OR PERCEPTION).

- OCCURRING INTERNALLY OR
INWARDLY.

6
"WHERE AM I GOING?"

What is my definite plan of action? Do I have a blueprint to follow? Would I travel to an unfamiliar city, or a foreign country without acquiring directions with which to navigate? No. Then how can I expect to go through life with no direction, no plan, no layout, no map?

Let me think about my PASSIONATE DESIRES for a moment . . . Now let me look at the accomplishments I've already made that spawned from those desires and see the possibilities for building on them.

I do not fear barriers, stumbling blocks, obstructions, snags, hindrances, difficulties, etc. Those all stem from a continual, doubtful mindset. They are those terrifying things fearful people see when they take their eyes off of their objectives.

PAS·SION·ATE
|ˈPA SH əNIT|
ADJECTIVE

- SHOWING OR CAUSED BY STRONG
FEELINGS OR A STRONG BELIEF.

- DOMINATED BY OR EASILY
AFFECTED BY INTENSE EMOTION.

I will devise and focus on the DESIGN of MY DESIRE. And I will do this by planning to the very end. I will write down my short and long term goals. I will enroll in classes if need be.

I will seek out all the particulars: news, instructions, statistics, timetables, etc. I will research and study the necessary information. I will find mentors who possess an appreciable level of expertise in my area of interest. I will set a deadline for myself and I WILL meet it.

I will use every tool made available to me so as to structure a layout that will guide me up the road to success.

I have put on my blinders and I know exactly where I am going. With that...

Put on your blinders.	• Envision exactly where you want to go.
Structure a layout.	• Your layout will guide you up the road to success.

TIMON KYLE DURRETT

DE·VISE |DIˈVĪZ|
VERB

- PLAN OR INVENT (A COMPLEX
PROCEDURE, SYSTEM, OR
MECHANISM) BY CAREFUL THOUGHT.

FO·CUS |ˈFŌKəS|
NOUN

- THE CENTER OF INTEREST OR
ACTIVITY.
VERB
- PAY PARTICULAR ATTENTION TO.

7

"WHAT WILL I DO TODAY TO ENHANCE AND ADVANCE MY LIFE AND THE LIVES OF THOSE AROUND ME?"

Today is a great day to improve myself. How? By passionately diving into what I love doing, and putting what and whom I love first - including myself. It is a surefire way to bring about the desired enhancements and advancements. I must remember that PASSION is a PREREQUISITE of ENHANCEMENT AND ADVANCEMENT, and EFFORT is a PREREQUISITE of PASSION. If I do not have passion, I do not have forward and upward progress.

To achieve excellence, I must develop passionate habits in ALL matters – big or small. Advancement is not a destination; it is an ongoing voyage in pursuit of the betterment of my total existence.

TIMON KYLE DURRETT

EN·HANCE |EN'HANS|
VERB

- INTENSIFY, INCREASE, OR
FURTHER IMPROVE THE QUALITY,
VALUE, OR EXTENT OF (SOMETHING).

AD·VANCE |əD'VANS|
VERB

- MOVE FORWARD, TYPICALLY IN A
PURPOSEFUL WAY.
- PROMOTE OR HELP THE
PROGRESS OF.

W T H D I T I A

In short, it is a chosen lifestyle. The more ACTIVELY PASSIONATE I am about who and what I love, the more happiness will find ME on my life's voyage.

Okay, I am certain of what I will do today.

That is why...

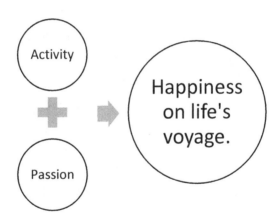

TIMON KYLE DURRETT

HAB·IT |ˈHABIT|
NOUN

- A SETTLED OR REGULAR
TENDENCY OR PRACTICE, ESP. ONE
THAT IS HARD TO GIVE UP.

EX·CEL·LENCE |ˈEKSələNS|
NOUN

- THE QUALITY OF BEING
OUTSTANDING OR EXTREMELY
GOOD.

8
"I DREAM BIG, ACT ON MY DREAMS, AND LIVE MY DREAMS!"

Everything great that ever happened was once a dream. But without "Action," a dream is nothing more than a wonderful thought.

It is a delightful, whimsical fantasy that will remain as such if I never put action behind it. Hoping and dreaming without action will leave me doing nothing more than HOPING and DREAMING.

So, if I want to better my life I must raise my standard of dreaming, acting, and living!

What if someone I admire thought small? What if he or she never took action beyond his or her dreams?

I may have never heard of that person.

TIMON KYLE DURRETT

DREAM |DRĒM|
NOUN

- A CHERISHED ASPIRATION,
AMBITION, OR IDEAL.

- AN UNREALISTIC OR SELF-
DELUDING FANTASY (IF ACTION
DOES NOT SUCCEED IT).

That person may have never touched and inspired my life and the lives of so many others.

See, that is what happens when I act on my dreams. The action not only changes me, but it can change each and every life I touch.

When I genuinely desire something, the whole universe works collectively to help bring my dream to fruition. The journey to destiny begins with desire.

As I Dream, Act and Live, I will also Be.

I dream BIG because…

As I
Dream.

As I
Act.

As I
Be.

TIMON KYLE DURRETT

HOPE |HŌP|
NOUN

- A FEELING OF EXPECTATION AND
DESIRE FOR A CERTAIN THING TO
HAPPEN.

VERB
- WANT SOMETHING TO HAPPEN
OR BE THE CASE.

W T H D I T I A

9
"WHO SAYS *I* CAN'T DO IT?"

In most cases, the answer to this question is ME. Saying "I CAN'T" is UNACCEPTABLE!

I HAVE enough in me to do ANYTHING I put MY MIND to. Just because my life has always been a certain way does not mean it has to always be that way. Life can be any way I want it to be, and it will not change unless I change.

I have the power to choose.

That being the case, instead of staying ruinously APATHETIC, I have become imaginatively COMMITTED.

Therefore, I free myself of the past and of those imposed, stringent ideals of how my life SHOULD be.
There is no middle ground, no stagnation. I am either living or dying, moving forward or moving backward, ascending to great heights or descending to the depths of the ordinary. In order to be an OUTWARD SUCCESS, I must first be an INWARD SUCCESS!

TIMON KYLE DURRETT

UN·AC·CEP·TA·BLE |ˌəNəKˈSEPTəBəL|
ADJECTIVE

- NOT SATISFACTORY OR
ALLOWABLE.

AP·A·THET·IC |ˌAPəˈΘETIK|
ADJECTIVE

- SHOWING OR FEELING NO
INTEREST, ENTHUSIASM, OR
CONCERN.

W T H D IT I A

Never again will I be afraid to demand the very best of myself and for myself. I am CAPABLE of ANYTHING! Therefore, I WILL NOT DOUBT MYSELF!

Doubt operates from lack, which connotes weakness, and is therefore unattractive.

Self-confidence operates from abundance, which connotes power, and is therefore attractive.

I operate from abundance because I AM SELF-CONFIDENT and I know I lack nothing! So, I attract to myself more of what I am.

Hence, NOTHING WILL stop me from achieving my goals because I am confident NOTHING CAN stop me!

Doubt, the unenlightened state of mind that it is, leads to fear, which leads to immobilization, which leads to complacency, which leads to sheer laziness. It would lead me to BELIEVE my dreams CAN'T be attained!

So, why would I ever build such a case against myself?

TIMON KYLE DURRETT

SUC·CESS |Səkˈsɛs|
NOUN

THE ACCOMPLISHMENT OF AN
AIM OR PURPOSE.
- A PERSON OR THING THAT
ACHIEVES DESIRED AIMS OR ATTAINS
PROSPERITY.

COM·MIT |Kəˈmɪt|
VERB

- PLEDGE OR BIND (A PERSON OR
AN ORGANIZATION) TO A CERTAIN
COURSE OF ACTION.

I have freed myself of any shred of DOUBT, and I KNOW my dreams WILL be attained.

I give rise to my day because I have elevated my thoughts from within the muck of DOUBT!

I cannot realize true prosperity with a doubtful mindset. Therefore, I only visualize favorable outcomes on the horizon of my life, and I consciously take willful actions based on my vision!

I have rid myself of doubt and I realize that I CAN DO IT.

Also…

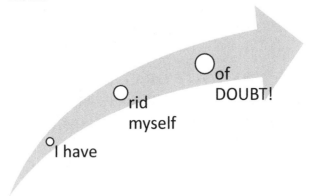

O of DOUBT!

O rid myself

O I have

TIMON KYLE DURRETT

LACK |LAK|
NOUN

- THE (MENTAL) STATE OF BEING
WITHOUT OR NOT HAVING ENOUGH
OF SOMETHING.

AB·UN·DANCE |əˈBƏNDƏNS|
NOUN

- THE STATE OR CONDITION OF
HAVING A COPIOUS QUANTITY OF
SOMETHING; PLENTIFULNESS.

- PLENTIFULNESS OF THE GOOD
THINGS OF LIFE; PROSPERITY.

W T H D I T I A

10
"I AM THANKFUL FOR EVERYONE WHO HAS EVER TOLD ME 'NO!'"

When someone tells me "No," I may have little to no influence over him or her, not yet anyway. But I do have control over what that "No" does to and for me.

When told "No," I can start the process of turning that negative into a positive by asking myself a simple, yet significant question: WHAT AM I WILLING TO DO TO GET A 'YES?'

I determine the toughness of my resolve by how many "No's" I can take. I do not let all those "No's" disappoint, deter, diminish, or devastate me! No. I use them as fuel, as my driving force to eventually get more "Yes's" than "No's."

TIMON KYLE DURRETT

THANK·FUL |ˈΘA NG KFəL|
ADJECTIVE

- PLEASED, EXPRESSING GRATITUDE
AND RELIEF.

WILL |WIL| |WIL|
NOUN

- THE FACULTY BY WHICH A
PERSON DECIDES ON AND INITIATES
ACTION.

- CONTROL DELIBERATELY EXERTED
TO DO SOMETHING OR TO RESTRAIN
ONE'S OWN IMPULSES.

- A DELIBERATE OR FIXED DESIRE
OR INTENTION.

Chopping down a giant tree can very well be a daunting task. I may not be able to do it in a day, in a week, or even in a month. But if I remove a mere splinter at a time from that tree, it will eventually fall.

It is because of each "No'" that I manage to get stronger.

The stronger the resolve, the greater the endeavor, the sweeter the end result, which will be a resounding "YES!"

I am thankful for the "No's." But I recognize some "No's" come from negative people, and...

TIMON KYLE DURRETT

RE·SOLVE |RIˈZÄLV; -ˈZÔLV|
VERB

– DECIDE FIRMLY ON A COURSE OF
ACTION.

NOUN
– FIRM DETERMINATION TO DO
SOMETHING.

11

"NEGATIVE PEOPLE STEAL FROM ME!"

When I look at a simple mathematic calculation (10 − 4 = 6, for example), I know that the minus symbol [-] literally means to "TAKE AWAY FROM."

It is the negative portion of the equation. Negative people will TAKE AWAY FROM ME if I allow them to, ideally making me part of THEIR EQUATION, which is to become EQUALLY as NEGATIVE as they are.

Navigating through life can be challenging enough without the burden of pessimistic, defeatist, critical people who opt for a "thumbs down" frame of mind.

It is much more pleasant to keep company with those who are like-minded and have my best interests at heart.

TIMON KYLE DURRETT

NEG·A·TIVE |ˈNEGəTIV|
ADJECTIVE

- (OF A PERSON, ATTITUDE, OR SITUATION) NOT OPTIMISTIC; HARMFUL OR UNWELCOME.

NOUN
- A WORD OR STATEMENT THAT EXPRESSES DENIAL, DISAGREEMENT, OR REFUSAL.

POS·SI·BLE |ˈPÄSəBəL|
ADJECTIVE

- ABLE TO BE DONE; WITHIN THE POWER OR CAPACITY OF SOMEONE OR SOMETHING.

W T H D I T I A

People who believe life is hard just may experience more hardships than people who believe ANYTHING IS POSSIBLE.

And those who believe ANYTHING IS POSSIBLE are more often met with more ease and comfort.

I do not let other peoples' fears distract me from my dreams. I have made positive changes. I have let go of those who loll about in negativity.

Life is too precious to put up with cynics.

If I can ever recall a time where I have told a friend, family member, co-worker, neighbor, significant other, or whomever, about my plans and the first thing he or she said was, *"Eh, I don't think that's a good idea,"* or *"Nah, that'll never work,"* then I must be careful not to share my aspirations with him or her again.

Besides, I do not need other people to validate my choices. My positive thoughts and beliefs create my life.

TIMON KYLE DURRETT

PES·SI·MIST|ˈPɛSəMəST|
NOUN

- A PERSON HAVING A TENDENCY
TO SEE THE WORST ASPECT OF
THINGS OR BELIEVES THAT THE
WORST WILL HAPPEN; HAVING A
LACK OF HOPE OR CONFIDENCE IN
THE FUTURE.

SAB·O·TAGE |ˈSABəˌTÄ ZH |
VERB

- DELIBERATELY DESTROY,
DAMAGE, OR OBSTRUCT
(SOMETHING).

There are too many people who refuse to do away with those negative mindsets and elevate themselves, which means they will inadvertently bring me down if I am not careful.

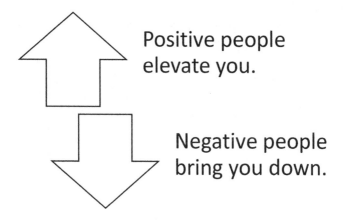

Positive people elevate you.

Negative people bring you down.

There are others who purposefully aim to demean my ambitions or sabotage my efforts. Either way, I continue to fly high and celebrate their criticisms and attempts to shatter my dreams because they only make me stronger.

I steer clear of negative people to avoid infection. Besides…

TIMON KYLE DURRETT

AS·PI·RA·TION |ˌASPəˈRĀ SH əN|
NOUN

- A HOPE OR AMBITION OF
ACHIEVING SOMETHING.

- THE OBJECT OF SUCH AN
AMBITION; A GOAL.

EL·E·VATE |ˈELəˌVĀT|
VERB

- RAISE OR LIFT (SOMETHING) UP
TO A HIGHER POSITION.

- RAISE TO A MORE IMPORTANT
OR IMPRESSIVE LEVEL.

12

"HOW DARE I EXPECT OTHERS TO BELIEVE IN ME IF I DON'T BELIEVE IN MYSELF?"

I will settle for ANYTHING if I do not BELIEVE in myself FIRST, and "ANYTHING" includes FAILURE.

If I do not expect proficiency and brilliance of myself, how can I expect others to? The only way I can excel is by facing and conquering my fears, which conquers doubt, which leads to and perpetuates genuine, enthusiastic BELIEF.

Wherever there is belief in my life, there are actions that follow. If I believe I will fail, more than likely my actions will lead to failure. If I believe I will win, more than likely my actions will lead to victory.

Powerful people sense fear and timidity. They can smell it a mile away.

TIMON KYLE DURRETT

FAIL·URE |ˈFĀLYəR|
NOUN

LACK OF SUCCESS.

- AN UNSUCCESSFUL PERSON,
ENTERPRISE, OR THING.

W T H   D   I T   I   A

So, even if they do not mean to, they will ignore, resent, or even crush me if I display such cowardice.

But the powerful can also sense confidence, which is one of the purest forms of life-enhancing BELIEF.

Such confidence will attract these very people to ME. They will come to BELIEVE in ME and expect as much greatness from ME as I do of myself.

Do I believe in myself? Absolutely!
For that reason…

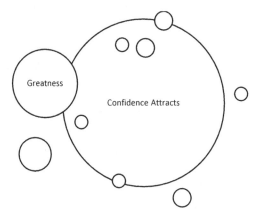

TIMON KYLE DURRETT

BE·LIEF |BIˈLĒF|
NOUN

- AN ACCEPTANCE THAT A
STATEMENT IS TRUE OR THAT
SOMETHING EXISTS.

- SOMETHING ONE ACCEPTS AS
TRUE OR REAL; A FIRMLY HELD
OPINION OR CONVICTION.

13

"I DO NOT WASTE TIME!"

As the old saying goes: The Mind Is A Terrible Thing To Waste. The same can be said about TIME.

If I find myself with "Free Time," but I have not reached my goals, then that time is not free. IT COSTS.

It costs me all-important opportunities that may never come knocking at my door again. It costs me my chances to achieve that which I want the most. It costs me PROSPERITY. It costs me my peace of mind. It costs me my happiness.

Dreams, desire, and talent by themselves will not cut it. Time waits for no one! I must utilize my time wisely. It is far too valuable for me not to do so.

I use my time effectively. Which means…

TIMON KYLE DURRETT

WASTE |WĀST|
VERB

- USE OR EXPEND CARELESSLY,
EXTRAVAGANTLY, OR TO NO
PURPOSE.

- BESTOW OR EXPEND ON AN
UNAPPRECIATIVE RECIPIENT.

- FAIL TO MAKE FULL OR GOOD USE
OF.

14

"I SHUT UP AND DO IT!"

Procrastination is the ugly cousin of laziness, and laziness is contagious and potentially long lasting. The only real difference between a procrastinator and a lazy person is one does not want to do it now; the other does not want to do it at all.

Taking action can be a life-changing thing.

One definitive, desire-based action toward a goal is far more powerful than a lifetime of merely talking about it. Show! Don't Tell!

If I were a boxer, would I tell my opponent what punches – or combination thereof – I was going to throw? Of course not. It would not have the same effect.

The same applies for continually blabbing on an on about what "I'm Gonna Do," but never having anything to show for all my TALKING.

TIMON KYLE DURRETT

PRO·CRAS·TI·NA·TION
|PRə͵KRASTə'NĀ SH əN; PRŌ-|
NOUN

- THE ACT OR QUALITY OF
DELAYING OR POSTPONING ACTION;
PUTTING OFF DOING SOMETHING.

AC·TION |'AK SH əN|
NOUN

- THE FACT OR PROCESS OF DOING
SOMETHING, TYPICALLY TO ACHIEVE
AN AIM.

W T H D I T I A

A bold, decisive action without hesitation has far greater effect than if words precede it.

I just SHUT UP AND DO IT. And I do it NOW! If I speak the words "I Want To…" from that point on ACTION IS MANDATORY.

It is simple: I can waste this moment or I can use it. Between those two choices lies a world of difference. By my ACTIONS, I make my life an accomplished one.

Great! I am DOING IT.

But the most important question is…

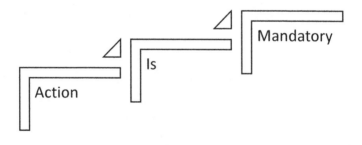

Action Is Mandatory

TIMON KYLE DURRETT

POW·ER·FUL |ˈPOU(-ə)RFəL|
ADJECTIVE

- HAVING GREAT POWER OR
STRENGTH.

- (OF A PERSON OR
ORGANIZATION) HAVING CONTROL
AND INFLUENCE OVER PEOPLE AND
EVENTS.

- HAVING A STRONG EFFECT ON
PEOPLE'S FEELINGS OR THOUGHTS.

15

"AM I SATISFIED?"

Am I truly content with who I am now that I have made these enhancements, or can I be more so? Am I ready and willing to hold my head high, walk with confidence, unashamed to proclaim to the world who and how I am right now?

I will not settle for "good enough." I will not think I have reached the end once I have achieved a definitive goal because I know there are more steps toward growth awaiting me.

I will adopt the mindset of a Champion, a Leader, a Creator, and a Doer.

The moment I BELIEVE I have DONE my BEST, I will DO BETTER. The moment I BELIEVE I am AT my BEST, I will GET BETTER.

TIMON KYLE DURRETT

A·MAZ·ING |əˈMĀZI NG |
ADJECTIVE

- CAUSING GREAT SURPRISE OR
WONDER; ASTONISHING.

- STARTLINGLY IMPRESSIVE.

W T H D I T I A

If I WANT AMAZING, I must THINK AMAZING THOUGHTS. If I am as GREAT as I SAY I am, then I have to PROVE IT and BE as GREAT as I SAY I AM.

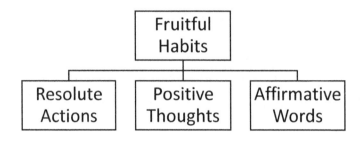

I WILL CONCEIVE ONLY POSITIVE THOUGHTS. I WILL GENERATE AFFIRMATIVE WORDS, WHICH LEAD TO PROMPT AND RESOLUTE ACTION. I WILL DEVELOP FRUITFUL HABITS SO THAT I WILL FASHION A FIRST-RATE CHARACTER AND FORGE MY EXTRAORDINARY DESTINY!

TIMON KYLE DURRETT

GREAT |GRĀT|
ADJECTIVE

- OF AN EXTENT, AMOUNT, OR
INTENSITY CONSIDERABLY ABOVE
THE NORMAL OR AVERAGE.

- OF ABILITY, QUALITY, OR EMINENCE
CONSIDERABLY ABOVE THE NORMAL
OR AVERAGE.

W T H D I T I A

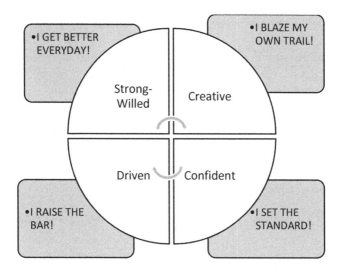

TIMON KYLE DURRETT

I AM: Strong-Willed Confident Assertive Fearless Intelligent Lion-Hearted Self-Motivated Active Driven Enthusiastic Beneficial Self-Sufficient Fortified Dynamic Positive Inspiring Studious Determined Self-Assured Passionate Brilliant Eager Creative Daring Worthy Clever Vigorous Formidable Sharp Self-Aware Awe-Inspiring Respectable Enlightened Upstanding Diligent Polite Gracious Admirable Tough Adventurous Focused Skillful Goal-Oriented Happy Dominant Resolute Insightful Prepared Perseverant Decisive Persuasive Reliable Perceptive Exuberant Vital Industrious Significant Productive Compassionate Successful Buoyant Talented Committed Thorough Trustworthy Willful Steadfast Inspirited Indomitable Zealous Proficient Commanding Grounded Composed Influential Enterprising Determined, and Powerful!

I KNOW
WHO THE HELL
I AM!

TIMON KYLE DURRETT

AHY NŌ
HOŌ Đə
HEL
AHY AM!

ABOUT THE AUTHOR

Timon is a passionate thinker and consummate dreamer.

The Chicago-born author, actor, and artist has long examined the idea of who we are as interactional beings. His fervent enthusiasm to find answers to what makes us tick steadily urges him further into this inquisition. Hence, the composition you now possess.

Timon encourages those who read his work to identify their truest potential and educe the very same from others. Unraveling one's self-mystery is a milestone everyone can reach.

For, to know oneself is true power.

Connect with Timon on Twitter @TimonKDurrett; and on Facebook.com/TimonKyleDurrett.

TIMON KYLE DURRETT

Special thanks to my soror Zondra Hughes and the Six Brown Chicks.

Made in the USA
Las Vegas, NV
15 December 2021